How To Shoot Your First Short Film On A PHONE

By

Steve Watson

ALH Publishing

11 The Woodwards

Newark, NG24 3GG

Cover designed by SWP Media

ISBN: 978-1-7393101-0-3

To all who have a passion
to tell something

INTRODUCTION

Let me start by saying that in this digital world we live in today, you have no excuse for not shooting or creating your first short film because, every day you carry around with you the most sophisticated and yet simple recording device that was once out of your reach. Today, all you need do is reach into your pocket or your bag and pull out the most exciting piece of equipment that has been created just for you…

YOUR PHONE

CONTENTS

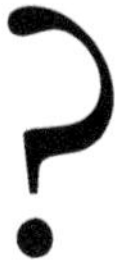

WHERE DO YOU BEGIN

Well, the first thing I did was to have an **idea**.

I suppose that does sound obvious, but there are some people out there that would just pick up their phones and just start shooting. Now that is exactly what I would **recommend you do.**

The fact is, you already know how to use your phone by snapping images every day and posting them on to some social media platform waiting for someone to like and share your images. And I am pretty sure that you are constantly videoing the family or friends, or just uploading those silly shorts to the likes of Tik Tok, trying to make you a **millionaire**.

Don't get caught up in all that stuff if what you really want to do is make a **short film.** That's not to say you shouldn't have a go at trying to make that killer Tik Tok, who knows it could just be your luck, and **Bang,** you land the big one.

In order to make life a lot **simpler**, I am going to take you through, **step by step,** on a project that I shot several years ago on my phone.

I didn't have the money to buy all the equipment that I was told I had to have in order to become a filmmaker, so I decided to look at a cheaper way and, in some sense, a more efficient way of shooting.

Now I know what you are thinking, this guy knows didley squat about filmmaking and here he is trying to tell us that he knows best.

Hear me out.

When I looked at all the equipment I needed: camera, lighting, sound, tripod, computer, hard drives, backup system, capture cards, the list just keeps on going and it was a fortune. It's not until now, because of the capabilities of the mobile phones, that all the above equipment has come down in price (not always the case when you are looking at top pro gear).

When you look at the device in your pocket, believe it or not, it has most of those things built in or the accessories are cheap enough for you to buy to make that killer film.

So, now you know that you have everything you need in your pocket, lets' get to your idea and start fleshing it out.

Remember, I said we would look at my short film and how I went about making it.

USE THIS PAGE TO WRITE DOWN SOME IDEAS

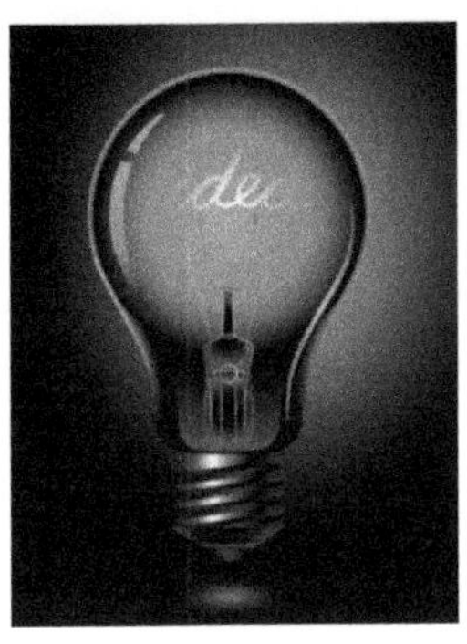

THE IDEA

When I started to think about what I wanted to film, it was a nightmare. How did I know what I wanted to shoot hadn't already been made.

The problem with ideas is, you may think you have an original idea, but when you do some research into your **genre,** or type of film you want to shoot, someone has already made it.

So, I would suggest trying out a few things first. It's no good jumping in at the deep end and then realizing that you have bitten off more than you can chew.

Start small.

Get use to using the camera and its functions. More about this in another chapter.

I wanted to shoot a sort of a comedy but with a dark twist to it. I wanted to make sure that whatever it was I was going to shoot, the audience would think one thing whilst another was taking place.

Let me elaborate.

I had this idea that a fella and his missus, who were now separated because he couldn't stand the sight of her or take anymore of her moaning, came up on the Lottery. This was a massive win.

Now the problem was, is he entitled to the money if they were split. In his eyes he was because it was him that went and bought the ticket. The problem for him is, although he went and bought the ticket; not with his own money, but from the money the wife gave him, he did not hold the winning ticket either. There was no way of him proving that it even existed.

Now I had a **dilemma**. How would this **scenario** sit in the eyes of the law, so I decided to do some **research.**

This is what I found out:

When relationships breakdown, what happens to that lottery windfall?

The starting point is to find out whether the couple are married or unmarried. There is a huge difference in how lottery wins are treated in law depending on your marital status.

Unmarried couples

If the couple are unmarried, then the general rule is that the person who bought the winning ticket and holds the winnings, is entitled to the windfall. It may appear unfair to many, but the reality is that the other party would have no claim against those winnings in the event of the breakdown of the relationship.

The exception is where, for example, the windfall has already been shared (gifted), placed in a joint bank account used by both parties, or invested in joint assets, such as home.

Where children are involved, it may be possible to make a claim against the lottery winner for financial provision for the benefit of that child – for example, to provide a home for the child, but once the child is grown up, the property will be returned to the lottery winner.

Married Couples or Civil Partners

Contrast this with married couples or civil partners. Upon divorce, the court will look very carefully at the windfall – even if it has been retained by the winner. All of the assets owned by each party must be disclosed and taken into consideration so as to enable the court to determine what is fair.

So, now knowing that there was going to be a problem with what I was proposing, was there another way that even though they were still married, and they had won the 'big one', was it possible to screw the husband out of the windfall? Afterall, the only reason he was back knocking on her door is because of that win

There was.

I decided to turn the whole idea on its head. If it meant, even though they were still technically married, even though they were separated, and he did buy the ticket which meant that they wouldn't have won if he hadn't bought the ticket, even if it was with her money and not his and the fact that he didn't have the ticket, but she did, why not lose the ticket altogether and devise a plan that she still comes out the **winner.**

And that is exactly what I did.

I now knew that I had an idea that was worth working on. I couldn't find any other short films along those lines.

So, the next thing I had to do was to create the **characters.**

I had decided that these two main characters were living in a semi-detached house. Both were working.

I didn't need to flesh these characters out too much with a backstory and all (this just mainly means who they are and where did they come from etc.) because we weren't getting in too deep with the story. We were only getting a small portion of the larger project. I only wanted to concentrate on one piece and this part of the story lent itself nicely to creating the short film.

Now, I had to flesh the whole thing out.

How did it start?

Was there a **voiceover** or did we get straight into the **dialogue** and the **action**. I deliberated for some time and thought I would start it from:

a blackout fade in and then a loud knocking at the front door. The wife was in bed. It was early morning, and it was the ex-banging on the door.

She gets out of bed, looks out the window and sees her ex pacing up and down.

To me, as it was a short, this was the perfect way to start the whole thing.

Here is the link for you to see the film on youtube:

I had the **beginning** of the film, but what was going to happen next.

Each step of the way the story needed to **flow**, so what was I going to do next?

I wanted the two of them to have a row about the winning lottery ticket. The wife remarks that he is more interested in the ticket than her.

"did you ever love me?" she wants to know. 'No", comes the reply.

Oh boy! This **plot** has now just got interesting. What happens next shouldn't be surprising.

Now agitated, the husband grabs the ex-wife and tells her to find the missing ticket.

"you're going to find that ticket or else,' screams the husband.

We now have a reason for het to set the **deceit** wheels in motion. After all, this was now a scorned woman. Watch out when you upset a woman, you never know what beast lies within.

Rather than make more of this scene, we **cut** to a new **location**. Here the two are in a coffee shop. The husband is already there waiting.

Another row breaks out because the ex-wife has kept him waiting. Once inside and sat down, the wife provokes him and shows him the ticket. She asks him if he had ever loved her at all and he replies,

'No'

to which she replies as she tears up the ticket,

'Then neither of us shall have it".

The husband screams as she tears it up into little pieces and laughs.

I did say that you should never upset a woman because you never know what will happen. (I must remember here that it was me that came up with this plot and not a woman)

How do I follow that scene because she has just cut short the whole film.

Remember me telling you that I turned the whole thing up on its head, well this is where it all makes sense for her outburst in the Coffee shop.

I decided to put myself in her shoes. What would I do if I didn't want my ex to get their hands on any of the **winnings?**

I **invented** a close friend of the couples, who had a printing company. He always liked the wife and when she told him that she wanted to play a trick on her ex-husband, he thought it hilarious and obliged by printing a copy of the ticket.

Now do you see what I did. I set up a **STING.**

But there was more to come.

HOW WAS SHE GOING TO GET AWAY WITH IT?

I decided that the only sensible **course of action** was to give the ticket to her mother. As far as the ex-husband knew, he had pissed the ex-wife off, and she had torn up the winning ticket in front him. Why should he think that the woman he had been married to all these years was capable of such a deceitful thing.

I'm not casting aspersions about women and their capabilities but let's just say the whole thing is better left alone. When you tie the knot and they hear those words,

"I Do,"

You basically gave up the right of being able to do anything you want, when you want, with whom you want.

NOW LET'S MOVE ON!

So, if Mum was given the ticket and she presented it to Camelot, who was to know that it wasn't hers Only one person for sure; the daughter and she wasn't going to say anything. The husband could be suspicious all he wanted. The truth is, he didn't pay for the ticket and then decided to end his pitiful life with his moaning wife all because he thought he had won the big one.

Life can be such a bitch at times.

Well, there you have it.

I had a **PLOT**

USE THIS PAGE AND THE NEXT TO CREATE A PLOT

USE SOME OF THE NOTES YOU MADE EARLIER

MAKE MORE NOTES HERE

AND HERE

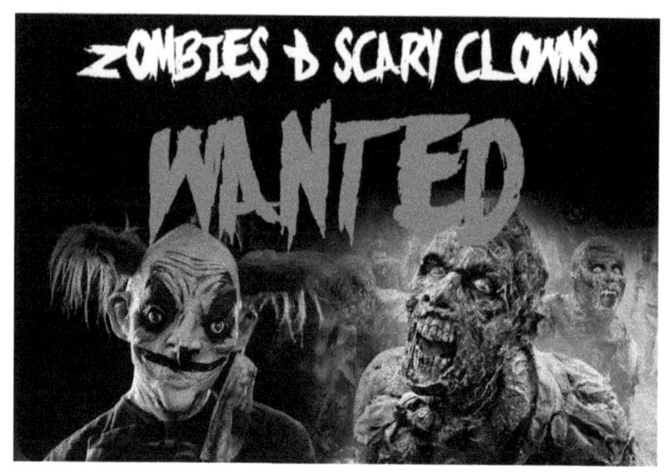

CHARACTERS

As it was one of my first short films, I basically wanted to keep things simple.

I knew I had to have at least three people in the film; wife, husband, and friend.

Now, this is not a book on film theory and thank heavens for that, because this could be filled with all sorts of stuff for you. I will at the end leave you with a website that is amazing for **FREE** information on filmmaking, if you are interested in taking it further.

Now, back to the characters.

I wanted to make sure that everyone could identify with **type** of characters I was going to put in the film.

A stroppy husband, a sensitive wife and a friend that likes a good laugh.

Now where was I going to get those type of characters?

Good news. I had a friend that was pretty good at **acting** and she could turn her hand to most things. Not that she is downtrodden or slightly sympathetic, oh no, this woman could cut the skin from a frozen fish with her tongue. But I knew that she could play the little wife if need be.

Great. One down, two to go. The husband had to be stroppy, cutting, a bit of a pig; I **cast** myself in that role. I wasn't sure that I could get someone with so many great qualities. I'm not advocating that I have them, I just knew I could play the part. I did write it after all.

Don't be afraid to take on a part if you

cannot find anyone to play it. Let's be fair, you know exactly how to play the role with all the **mannerisms** and **attitude**. Get in front of the camera and show them what you can do. It is very uplifting and fun.

The third character, a friend who like a bit of a laugh. Remember, he also had to be a business owner, so he had to have a little something about him. Lucky for me, I had just the friend.

He was a businessman, very funny, cheeky smile and perhaps his most endearing quality, he looked like Shrek!

I know. What would be the chances of finding a person with a face like Shrek's. He does really make you laugh.

Anyway. Now all three characters were **identified**, I had to approach them and ask if they were **interested** in taking part in the shoot. Luckily for me, all three wanted to take part.

Now, just a point of interest here.

If you were going to enter the short film into

a Film Festival or try and sell the idea on, you would have to get the people taking part to sign a contract. I'm not going to go into any of that here, but you would have to think about it if you were.

I didn't get any of them to sign a contract because I was just finding my feet and wanted to use this experience as a test bed.

I will leave a link and a sample template at the end of the book for you.

Ok, so I have my cast, but there are still a few things I needed to clear up.

What were they going to wear?

Luckily for me, I had **set** the film in the **modern day**. Like, now.

That meant that I could just get them to wear their usual clothes for lounging around the house, out during the day or at work. **Simple.**

Now there is a lesson here. Keep it SIMPLE.

Unless you are doing a period piece, some

sci-fi, western or whatever, for your first attempt, write what you know and set the film in places you can get access to.

WRITE DOWN YOUR IDEAS ABOUT YOUR CHARACTERS

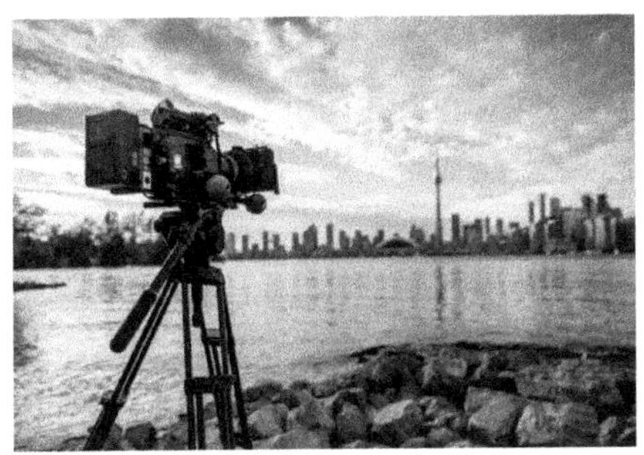

LOCATION

There is one thing you need to be aware of when choosing **locations** and that is, make sure for your first shoot, if not for all your shoots, that all the **locations** are within easy distance of each other.

Why do we do this?

It's just to make **filming easier**.

On my film, I made sure that the bedroom scene and the kitchen scene were shot in one location.

Remember I said that they lived in a semi-detached house, well, one of the **cast** actually was willing to let us use their house.

I did make sure beforehand, by going up to the house and doing a **recce** (what I mean by recce is a look). Make sure you check out every location that you decide on. If other members of the cast can't make it (you don't need them to see it until the day of the shoot if necessary) take a snapshot and put it up on a social page that you have set up.

Again, when making a film for **distribution** or the bigger **film festivals** you would need to have a **location release form**. This just protects the person's property and lets them know that you will take full responsibility if any damage occurs.

The coffee shop was a different kettle of fish. I needed to make sure that the place was big enough for me to film in. The other thing I needed to make sure, was that no one would be using the place whilst I was filming; the general public I mean. You need to be able to **control** the whole environment. You don't want people shouting, talking, or ordering cups of tea and coffee just as you start to film.

I was lucky in the fact that I had a friend who owned a coffee shop, and they gave me **permission** to use the place whilst it wasn't in use.

Because the shots I required were mainly **Medium Close Ups** (more on the types of shots later) I could control exactly what was going to be in the **frame.** Every shot I wanted also had a **shallow depth of field** (that basically means the background was out of **focus**).

I also needed someone in the coffee shop to serve the teas and coffees. I took a chance and asked my friends wife if she would like to play the barista. She jumped at the chance.

You will be surprised at the amount of people that want to take part in a **short film**. It's their way of getting that fifteen minutes of fame.

Sometimes, you will be surprised at what your friends can do for you. In my case, these guys were all up for **acting** and lending me their locations to shoot.

Now, one of the issues I had was how to shoot the friend of the husbands. Remember, he was the Printer. I looked at different scenarios and decided the only way I would get away with it was to shoot outside a printer's shop. I would show the shop but have all the dialogue spoken outside it and in a **wide shot** (once again, I will go over these different types of shot later in its own chapter).

I did however, just to be **courteous**, let the owner of the shop know that I would be filming outside his premises. He wanted to know what the scene was about, and it wasn't until I had told him what the scene entailed, did he give me **permission**.

Some people can be finicky, so beware, some may ask you to move on politely or be an absolute arse about it.

You can shoot in the streets ideally without a tripod without consent. As soon as you set a tripod down, in some cases, you are going to need to get **permission** and have **public liability and personal liability insurance** in place.

Shooting handheld is generally named as

'guerilla shooting' or **'shooting on the fly'**.

Shooting in this **style** allows you to get in and out of areas or situations quickly to get the **shots** you require.

Make some notes on what you require from your location

And here

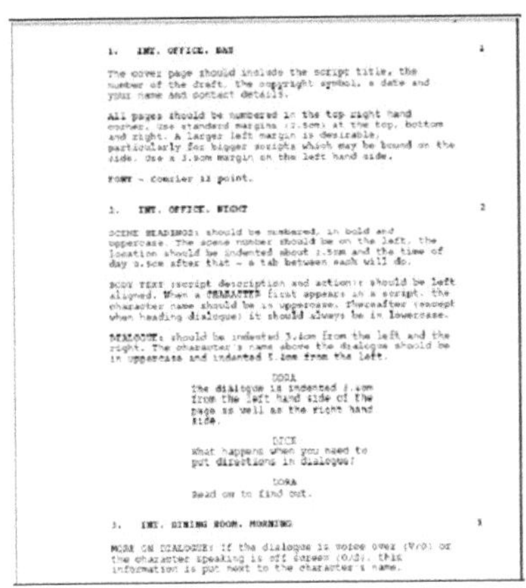

1. INT. OFFICE. DAY 1

The cover page should include the script title, the number of the draft, the copyright symbol, a date and your name and contact details.

All pages should be numbered in the top right hand corner. Use standard margins ([illegible]) at the top, bottom and right. A larger left margin is desirable, particularly for bigger scripts which may be bound on the side. Use a [illegible] margin on the left hand side.

FONT - Courier 12 point.

2. INT. OFFICE. NIGHT 2

SCENE HEADINGS: should be numbered, in bold and uppercase. The scene number should be on the left, the location should be indented about [illegible] and the time of day [illegible] after that - a tab between each will do.

BODY TEXT (script description and action): should be left aligned. When a **CHARACTER** first appears in a script, the character name should be in uppercase. Thereafter (except when heading dialogue) it should always be in lowercase.

DIALOGUE: should be indented [illegible] from the left and the right. The character's name above the dialogue should be in uppercase and indented [illegible] from the left.

DORA
the dialogue is indented [illegible] from the left hand side of the page as well as the right hand side.

DICK
What happens when you need to put directions in dialogue?

DORA
Read on to find out.

3. INT. DINING ROOM. MORNING 3

MORE ON DIALOGUE: If the dialogue is voice over (V/O) or the character speaking is off screen (O/S), this information is put next to the character's name.

SCRIPT

A **script** I hear you cry. I've never written a script.

Now don't worry yourself about the way a script should be laid out. This is your first attempt at **shooting a short film.**

You may decide to not use any **dialogue**. You may wish to use very little dialogue. It maybe that the whole short film is **voiced over**. Whatever it is, don't worry too much about it.

I will show you a **sample script** later in the book for those of you who would like to know how to lay one out.

What I did was to break each scene down and think about what each person was going to say.

As I mentioned at the beginning of the book, we open on a **black fade up** and the sound of knocking then straight into the imagery. We see the wife clamber from the bed confused as to who could be knocking at 6am in the morning.

Let me show you how I set this out on some A4.

I did, once I had the A4, I knew that I had to set the time of day and whether it was an interior shot or an exterior shot and the location.

SAMPLE SCRIPT

The scene **fades in** and we hear a loud knocking sound coming from the front door.

INT. BEDROOM. EARLY MORNING

SFX: knocking from front door

A voiceover or **V.O**: you wouldn't want to be woken by that row first thing in the morning.

Cut to: the ex-wife looks at the clock

Cut to: clock showing 6.00

Cut to: ex-wife clambering out of bed

EX-WIFE: who the hell could that be at this time in the morning

She gets out of bed and goes to the window. She notices her ex-husband pacing up and down

EX-WIFE: It's Dave. What the bloody hell does he want?

Now the layout I have shown you is not the correct layout that the industry uses, but let's face it, it tells you everything you need to know, do and say.

I did, however, type the script up into an industry format later. The actors I was using were used to a script as they had both been on the stage and use to a certain layout although there is a difference between a TV or Film script and a Stage Play.

Now there is no reason why you can't just go out and start to film, because let's face it, you have now got the **actors**, **locations** and we know what **period** it is set in, which will determine the style of clothes they are wearing, and that you are going to shoot everything **handheld** outdoors on the street. Everything indoors, you can use a **tripod** to your hearts content.

Obviously, by using a tripod the shots are going to be steadier (you can use a device in the editing program to steady up the shakiness of the shot, but that's for another chapter).

USE THIS PAGE TO WRITE A SAMPLE SCRIPT

USE THIS PAGE TO WRITE A SAMPLE SCRIPT

USE THIS PAGE TO WRITE A SAMPLE SCRIPT

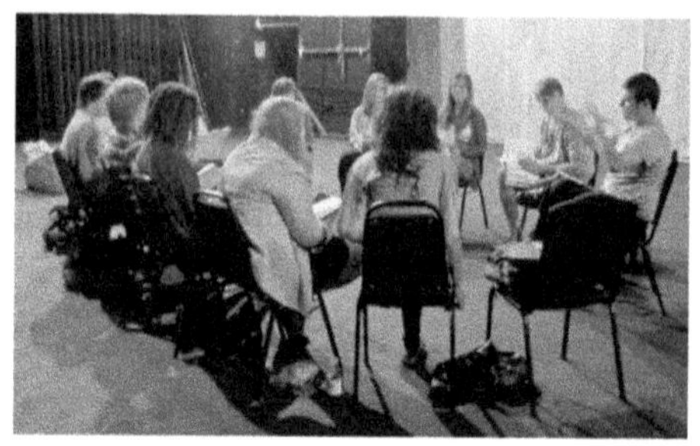

READ THROUGH

Ok, so we now have everything in place for our little shoot. What would be the next step do you think in making sure that everyone knows their lines?

That's right, a Read Through or a Rehearsal.

What I did was to have regular meetings. That way I was sure that we were not going to waste time when we got to the shoot.

It was only once a week for a few weeks. Because the **script** was short, each **scene** lasted no more than a couple of minutes.

Usually, one page is about one minute of time. It's an easy gauge that the industry relies on or so's they say.

It's not a bad gauge or tool to know because it does help when you are writing your **scrip**t.

How do you do a read through?

I make sure that when I do my **read throughs**, I'm either at home or I have hired a room somewhere in town. Equally, if one of the actors is single or has a room you can use, just to sit and read the script, I would take that option as it has cost you nothing and let's face it, some places are **not cheap to hire**.

When it comes to **running** or **blocking scenes**, I do recommend a larger space for you to move in.

It is a good idea for you to have **measured up** the location you are going to use to make sure that not only the actors can fit, but the **production crew** too.

A little on this point of production crew. It is possible to shoot your short all on your own if you are just making it for fun. And that is not to say that you couldn't shoot it on your own for real, but you would have to take in to account some other factors; sound being one of them.

Now, your phone is sophisticated, and the audio pick up on them these days is pretty good. This means that you become the **Cameraperson** and the **Sound person** all in one. (a **single person shoot**).

One thing to remember when **shooting** and **recording sound,** is, do not cover the **mic** with your hand; it will muffle the sound.

There are options for you. You could **invest** in an **external mic** and a **boom pole**, or you could buy a mic that fits directly to your phone.

Amazon is a great place to get all your kit from if you need anything. It convenient just to type in the search area – **Rode mic** for (whatever make your phone is). Most of the attachments for the sound are through **'stereo jack mics.** If you have the budget, you could get the boom pole attached to an **audio recorder**, but these are a little pricey.

You may also want to consider a **'RIG'**, to hold your phone in. I managed to pick one up for a little as £6 from guess where. **AMAZON**.

The 'RIG' was great. It held the camera in place and allowed me to move as one unit.

What do I mean by that?

I mean, when I needed to **create a pan**, I grasped with both hands the rig and started to move from left to right and when I wanted to **create a tilt**, I would move the rig from top to bottom.

I will give you more info on types of shots in another chapter.

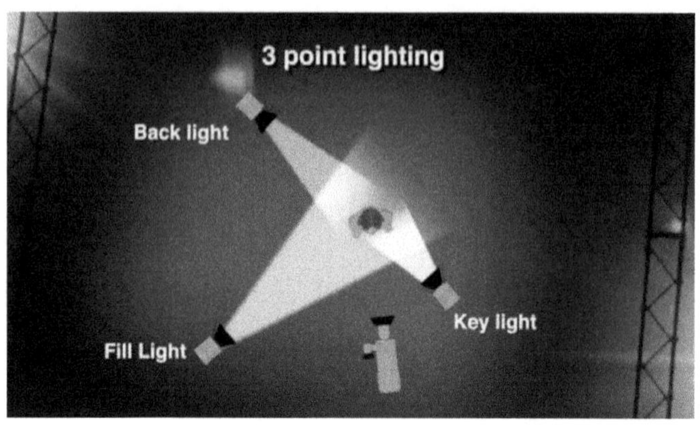

LIGHTING

I prefer to shoot my stuff with **natural light**. I don't tend to add any light into a **scene**. Now some people will tell you that that is crazy. I like to have a natural feel to the stuff I shoot. If at some point, there is not enough light for me to shoot the scene and I really need it, I will then think about putting in a small kick of light.

The issue you have when you introduce light into the equation, it's usually this section of the **production** that takes time to set up and get right.

When I shot in the kitchen for the short film, there was a huge window to the side which gave me both side light and main light when I needed it. There was also the window at the other end of the kitchen. This again was invaluable as it gave me two light sources from different angles and allowed me to rim light the character when needed.

I did, as you will see in the film, turn on the kitchen light just to give it a lift, but I haven't gone out my way to introduce some huge light boxes or even **LED** stand lights to illuminate the kitchen.

When the chap was sat on the stall looking at this wife, we had both windows throwing enough light into the room to light the scene.

And that was pretty much it for the lighting needed to do what I needed it to do.

Now, the **interior** shot in the Coffee shop was even easier. It had if you noticed a huge window that I sat both **characters** next to. There was so much light it created a beautiful **wrap around light**. There was no need to inject any other lighting.

The **exterior** shot outside the printers was **all-natural light.** It too provided me with everything I needed. It would have been a nightmare to have been setting lights up in the street. Now, then we would have needed **permissions** and **permits.**

The whole shoot was easy in terms of lighting, sound, and shooting.

We are not going to get hung up here about **bounce boards** or **reflectors**. Just know at this time, they are used to kick light into a scene. Because this is our first
crack at shooting a film, just keep it simple. We can explore more technical stuff in another book.

If you do decide to shoot night scenes, think carefully about how you create or provide your light for the scene and the character.

MAKE A LIST OF LIGHTING YOU THINK YOU MIGHT NEED

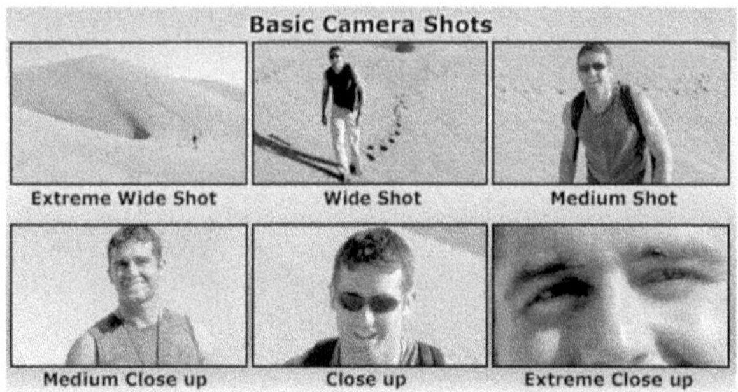

TYPES OF SHOTS

When you watch the TV, there are only a handful of shots that are used unless you have a fancy **director** who is hell bent on creating weird and wonderful shots.

For my short film, I thought about what I wanted the audience to experience when they looked at the screen.

You will notice that I opened with an **establishing shot** (that shows most of the room). It set the scene up and gave us a place – the bedroom.

I used **a wide shot** for the entrance of the husband. You could argue that that shot was also an establishing shot because we cut to another location.

When I needed to create a little **tension**, I changed the shot to a **medium close up**, like, when the husband grabs her arms and threatens her. I used the same shot in the Coffee shop when the two were talking about the Lottery ticket.

I just need to make sure that this first attempt of filming something was straight forward.

Most of the time, the scenes were shot in **wide shots** or **medium close ups**.

Types of Camera Shot Sizes

The Different Types of Shots

1. Extreme Wide Shot (ELS)
2. Long Shot (LS) / Wide Shot (WS)
3. Full Shot (FS)
4. Medium Long Shot (MLS) / Medium Wide Shot (MWS)
5. Cowboy Shot
6. Medium Shot (MS)
7. Medium Close Up (MCU)
8. Close Up (CU)
9. Extreme Close Up (ECU)
10. Establishing Shot

Let's take a look at the way these shots are described.

It all starts with an establishing shot

An **establishing shot** is a shot at the head of a scene that clearly shows us the location of the action. Sometimes an **aerial shot** will be used and is used to show where everything will happen.

Extreme Long Shot (ELS) or Extreme Wide Shot (EWS)

An **extreme long shot** (or **extreme wide shot**) makes your subject appear small against the location. You can use an extreme long shot to make your subject feel distant or unfamiliar.

It can also make your subject feel overwhelmed by its **location**. Of all the various **camera shots**, consider using the **extreme long shot** when you need to emphasize the location or isolation.

Long Shot (LS) or Wide Shot (WS)

The long shot (also known as a **wide shot**, abbreviated "**WS**") is the same idea, but a bit closer. If your subject is a person, then their whole body will be in view — but not filling the shot.

In other words, there should be a good deal of space above and below your subject. Use a **long shot** (or **wide shot**) to keep your subject in plain view amidst grander surroundings.

The wide shot also lets us see the background view, as well as the onlookers which will make any big moment more **cinematic**.

Of the many camera shots, a long shot gives us a better idea of the scene setting and gives us a better idea of how the character fits into the area.

Full Shot (FS)

This shot let's your subject **fill the frame** while keeping emphasis on scenery.

The **full shot** can also be used to feature

multiple characters in a single shot.

Medium Wide Shot (MWS)

A medium long shot frames the subject from roughly the **knees up**. It splits the difference between a **full shot** and a **medium shot.**

Cowboy Shot (CS)

A variation on this is the Cowboy Shot, typically American, which frames the subject from roughly **mid-thighs up**. It's called a **"cowboy shot"** because it is used in Westerns to frame a gunslinger's gun or holster on his hip. So, make sure you use one of them shots if you are shooting a Cowboy Film.

Medium Shot (MS)

What camera shots reveal your subject in more detail?

The medium shot is one of the most common camera shots. It's like the cowboy shot above, but frames from roughly the **waist up and through the torso.** So, it emphasizes more of your subject while keeping their surroundings visible.

Medium shots may seem like the most standard camera shot around, but every shot size you choose will **influence** the viewer. A **medium shot** can often be used as a buffer shot for dialogue scenes that have an important moment later that will be shown in a **close-up shot.**

If you don't use all of the different types of camera shots in a film, how can you **signal** anything to your **audience** without varying the **shot size.**

Medium Close Up Shot (MCU)

The medium close-up frames your subject from roughly the **chest up**. So, it typically favours the face, but still keeps the subject somewhat distant.

Close Up (CU)

When you want to reveal a **subject's emotions and reactions,** use a close-up shot. The **close-up** camera shot fills your **frame** with a part of your subject. If your subject is a person, it is **often their face**.

Of all the different types of **camera shot** sizes in film, a **close-up** is perfect for **important moments.** The **close-up shot** size is near enough to register **tiny emotions**, but not so close that we lose **visibility**.

Extreme Close Up (ECU)

Want to emphasize a specific feature of your subject then Use an **ECU.**

An **extreme close up** is the most you can fill a frame with your subject. It often shows eyes, mouth etc. In **extreme close-up** shots, smaller objects get detail and are the **focal point**.

Shot size is the building block for choosing **camera shots**, but you'll also need to consider how **framing, focus** and **movement** can add **deeper meaning** to your shots.

Types of Camera Shot Framing

WORKING WITH CHARACTERS IN THE FRAME

1. Single Shot
2. Two Shot
3. Three Shot
4. Over-the-Shoulder Shot (OTS)
5. Point-of-View Shot (POV)

What is camera shot framing?

Camera shot framing is the art and science of placing subjects in your shots. Camera shots are all about **composition.** Rather than pointing the camera at the subject, you need to **compose** an image.

Single Shot

This is when your shot captures just one subject.

Single shots can be set and **framed** in any shot size you like, just as long as there is only one character **featured** within the frame.

Two Shot or 2-Shot

This is a camera shot with two characters featured in the same frame:

These shots are often really useful for allowing performances to play out in a single take.

Three Shot or 3-Shot

There is no prize here for guessing how many people are in the frame. That's right, **it** features three characters in the frame:

This next shot is one that I used in the Coffee shop Scene. It's the **Over the Shoulder shot**.

Over-The-Shoulder Shot (OTS)

If you consider the **perspective** of the shot from a **character's perspective**, then using an **over the shoulder shot** shows your subject from behind the shoulder of another character. Because it emulates **perspective**, it's common in conversation scenes.

DRAW THE 6 TYPES OF SHOTS

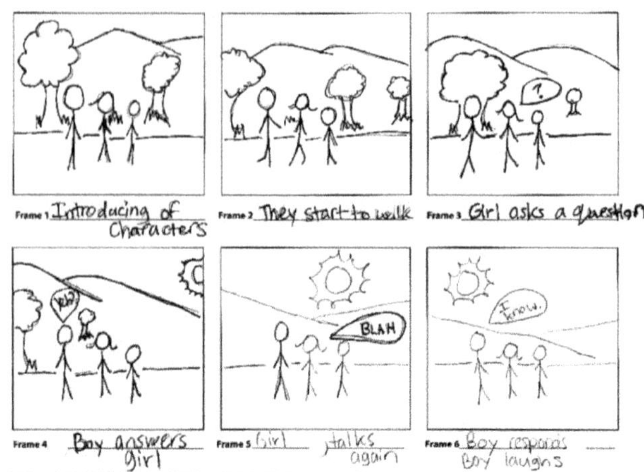

STORYBOARDING

I also used a **storyboard** to help with the **continuity** of **filming.** It was just a range of boxes; 6 to a page with enough space underneath to add some **dialogue**.

This just helped me as I went along and was able to know what I was **shooting** and how I wanted it to look.

The idea behind the **storyboard** is to give the **director** and the **cameraperson** an idea of what it is they are looking to create. This also helps the **editor** when you start to put your story together.

I went through the script page by page and then in my mind's eye, I created the shot I wanted to use. I then transferred the image on to the paper. I also made a note of the start of the line of dialogue and added that underneath the image.

I tried not to complicate the whole process and kept the shots simple at first. I mixed up the types of shots to make sure that the screen was changing, not too often, but enough to keep the audience interested.

STUDIOBINDER is my go-to site for everything relating to Film making.

Here is the web address: **studiobinder.com.**

Make sure you register and fill in all the details. I cannot tell you how useful this site is.

When you decide that you want to be a little more serious and maybe shoot something longer, with a budget and a team of people, the information on this site is what you want.

USE THIS SPACE TO DRAW UP A STORYBOARD OF A SCENE YOU HAVE IN MIND IN 8 SHOTS

SHOT 1

DIALOGUE HERE

SHOT 2

DIALOGUE HERE

SHOT 3

DIALOGUE HERE

SHOT 4

DIALOGUE HERE

SHOT 5

SHOT 6

SHOT 7

SHOT 8

You don't have to be a great drawer, just use stick men if need be or take photos of a scene whilst you are setting everything up; place your actors in position and then create the shot you want.

FREE STUFF

You can find a whole manor of **FREE** information, software, videos etc. on the web, but where are they and how do you access them?

Well, I'm going to make your life easy. I'm going to list out for you several of the sites and links that I use when I want to know something.

I always use **YOUTUBE**, because this is like the best resource station ever. Anyone who is anyone has posted up on this site and there is so much content, **FREE** content to be had.

It is also an excellent training platform. So, if you are just starting out, type in the search bar: **How to shoot Video on a phone**

You will see a whole host of sites to go on. The one that I recommend is:

10 Mobile Videography Tips For Beginners

By Learn online Video with Steve Wright

This is a great resource, and it is in simple language. Everything the guy talks about, and shows will make you a better filmmaker and he has probably saved you thousands in either not going to university or all those training courses that you can spend a pretty penny on.

How to Film like a PRO with Android Smartphones [Updated Guide!]

Justin Brown from Primal Video is another trainer that you should definitely check out on **YouTub**e.

When it comes to all the other stuff you need to do with your video, like: storyboard, script, production schedules, create calls sheets, then you definitely want to go to **STUDIOBINDER.COM.**

They also have a range of **FREE** tutorials for you to watch and learn from. Once again, this site is a **must for you**.

Now go and type in this into **YouTube**:

How to Make Your First Short Film: A Crash Course

Kent Lamm, from the Standard Story Company does a fantastic job of explaining what you should do if you are just starting out and want to make your first short film. Hence the title above.

If you want to take things a lot further and really get your teeth into the industry, there is a lot more that you should know when it comes to creating a film.

Want to produce a short film? Copy me.

The above title is what you need to type in to **YouTube** again, see, I told you it was a fantastic resource. Kent Lamm, gives a great run through on how to produce a short and what is involved.

So, we have looked at **Producing** and getting started what about scripting?

How to write a script for a short film are the only words you need to type into the search engine on, what platform? That's right, **YouTube** again.

You will find a host of videos all vying for your tender touch and to engage with their channel. Look for:

How To Write A Short Story Script

by Top Development.

Now, our friend explains that he did not write the script or make the film. What he has done, is deconstructed the whole thing for you. And what a great way of making a point. He makes sure you understand the **fundamental elements of a story** by using Dan Harmon's "Story Circle".

Everything about this video is well executed and will leave you feeling very confident.

Another great video on **YouTube**, again, is by our friend Top Development. In this Video he explains about:

How To Write Dialogue

What he does is break with normal conventions and gets it down to two defining points;

Focus on the purpose of the scene

Focus on making your characters sound natural and fluid

This all happens around **the 8-minute mark** just in case you don't want to listen to what else he has to say, which is a shame, because he makes some valid points.

Writing a script is the fun part, but you need to know what to do and how to do it. Once again, another **FREE** resource is my go-to place, as I mentioned before:

STUDIOBINDER

Only this time you need to go to the main page; **Studiobinder.com** and then in the search bar, type, **How To Write A Script.**

This will take you to a page that will give you three choices -

> **How to Write a Script Outline for Film and TV** (Free Template and Examples)
>
> But, just like any form of writing, you have to know where you're going first. Organization is important. That's where a **script**

outline comes into play. Understanding your central **character's desire**, and capturing the **scenarios** they attract for themselves, should guide that process.

There is no straightforward way to know how to **outline a screenplay**. But these tried-and-true guidelines will help you crack the structure for your character's journey.

How To Write A Short Film Script Without Dialogue

There are plenty of reasons why someone might want to keep dialogue out of their **short film** from stylistic choices to **technical limitations**. Here you will get to know all of the necessary steps to write a **short film script** without **dialogue** from research through execution.

How to Write a Character Breakdown for a Script — Pro-

Tips

Character breakdowns are important documents for **writers, casting agents, and actors**. Essentially, they're one-stop shops for **character details** and potential **shooting schedules**.

You will also find on this page a whole host of other **templates** and information all relating to your new interest.

When it comes to **editing** your project, you have a number of options. If you are on a **mac**, you have your built in **iMovie**. On the **PC**, you have your **Windows Movie Maker.**

Other options are:

HitFilm: A Free Video Editor That You Can Upgrade

HitFilm has lots of features anyone will love.

Some of the more advanced capabilities like **chroma key and picture-in-picture** will cost you, but they're decently priced. Plus, there's still a lot to like with this free **video editor**, even if you never buy an add-on.

Some of **Hit Films'** best features include the ability to auto-save as frequently as every minute, its dozens of keyboard shortcuts, colored labels (for **3D effects**, text, models, **composite shots**, images, and more), and the option to crop a clip and animate it to control which part is visible. You can also set a custom maximum undo level, access several default template options including **1080p Full HD**, mix and balance audio, use a helpful select tool to grab everything before or after the play head, and add unlimited video and audio tracks.

This free video editor was designed for **Windows 10 64-bit** and **macOS 11, 10.15, and 10.14**. The minimum **RAM** requirement is **8 GB.**

DaVinci Resolve is my absolute favourite editing software.

It is one of those unusual pieces of **video editing software**: fully featured, extremely powerful, yet **completely free**.
DaVinci Resolve is a tough app to beat. It's incredibly powerful, it's updated regularly, and to top it all, it's **FREE** It puts a lot of competing software to shame. The only downside is so much power leads to a complex interface.

But if you're serious about **video editing**, this shouldn't overwhelm you, and you're perfectly capable of sticking to the **Cut and Edit** pages for instance, leaving the more difficult pages for a later time. They'll still be there when you're ready for them.

All of my short films have been edited on **DaVinci Resolve,** because you can make it as simple as you want or really get to grips with it and do all sorts of editing tricks.

I could just keep on giving you tons of FREE stuff, but the most important thing here, is that you make a start on your own Short Film.

You have all the tools you require to at least

make a start.

All the items in this book I have either watched or read. There is so much out there for you to make that idea a reality.

The idea behind the book was to give first time Filmmakers some basic tools in order to get their short film made.

I've taken the years of experience that I have had in the industry and laid them down in a simplistic format for the filmmaker to understand. I know when I was starting out, how difficult it was to find help. So, to address the situation, I have laid out a simple follow me guide and applied it to a short film that was filmed on a phone.

I take you through a number of steps; where to begin, the idea, characters, location, script, the read through, lighting, types of shots, storyboarding and FREE STUFF. All of these elements are the building blocks in order to making a short film. I have only briefly touched on all these topics as we could get bogged down in academic formulas and techniques. I just want you to pick the phone up and with a little bit of knowledge, create that first short film. I know that once you have the first one down, you will want to start the second.

I will be creating a range of books that tackle a whole host of subjects all to do with filmmaking. They will be like little self-help books that will give you an insight to the filmmaking process. We can go into more depth on, what to do when you have made your film, how to edit it and the best software to use, how to submit to a festival, what formats your film needs to be in, how to shoot like a pro and much more.

But for now, GET SHOOTING!

JUST TO RECAP ON SOME OF THE FREE ITEMS

If you remember, I spoke about Studiobinder. This is my go-to platform if I need to know anything about making a film. It really is a one stop shop for everything filmmaking.

When it comes to the editing part, as I mentioned, once again, my go to platform is Davinci Resolve. It has everything you need to create some amazing films. It is busting at the seams with all sorts of effects, sound and colourization tools.

If you need some specific training on DaVinci they have that covered also.

FOR EVETRYTHING ELSE TRAINING WISE GO TO

ABOUT THE AUTHOR

As a child I was always acting and singing. I loved school and through myself into any production I could. I wasn't bothered what part it was, just as long as I could perform. As the years went by, I wanted to do more performances and eventually go to London to Drama School. It was the seventies and my dad said I had to get a proper job, so that never happened. My dream stayed with me until I became an extra on programs like, Tomorrows World, Crime Watch UK and Peak Practice. I also did a stint on a film, Signs and Wonders. I suddenly had a taste of TV and the big screen. I watched closely at what happened on these programs and thought I can do this. Pretentious I know, but I set up my own Production Company and started to make corporate films, which led into Short Films. I became a writer, Director, Producer and Filmmaker. One of the first things I made was when I was teaching and ran a summer school for kids. It was called from **Script To Screen**.

From

Script to Screen

An exciting new course for beginners

They had to come up with an idea, script it and then film it. They all wanted to be in it, so I had to do all the filming and then the editing. It was fantastic. Today I still teach and run courses, here and in France and America.

If you would like to attend one of my courses, you can email me on –

swatsonphotography@mac.com

How to use the QR Codes

Open the camera app on your smart phone, then hold the camera over the QR code on the page.

Once the camera has read the QR code, it will open a web link, just like below. Click on that link to be taken to YouTube to listen to the recording of the story.

www.ingramcontent.com/pod-product-compliance
Ingram Content Group UK Ltd.
Pitfield, Milton Keynes, MK11 3LW, UK
UKHW020226250726
13967UKWH00001B/208

9 781739 310103